SCHOLASTIC

FIRST COMPREHENSION:
NONFICTION

25 Easy-to-Read Informational Pages With Just-Right Questions

IMMACULA A. RHODES

New York • Toronto • London • Auckland • Sydney
Mexico City • New Delhi • Hong Kong • Buenos Aires

Cover design: Tannaz Fassihi; photo: © ImagesBazaar/Getty Images; illustration: Jannie Ho
Interior design: Michelle H. Kim; Interior illustration: Miguel Diaz Rivas/Advocate Art Inc.

Scholastic Inc., 557 Broadway, New York, NY 10012
ISBN: 978-1-338-31432-8
Copyright © 2019 by Scholastic Inc.
All rights reserved.
Printed in the U.S.A.
First printing, January 2019.

2 3 4 5 6 7 8 9 10   40   25 24 23 22 21 20

Contents

Biography

Introduction

Welcome to *First Comprehension: Nonfiction!* The 25 science, social studies, and biographical stories in this collection were developed to boost reading comprehension skills. The easy-to-read tales include repetition, decodable and high-frequency words, predictable patterns, and picture clues to aid in fluency so children can focus on the meaning of what they read. Reproducible comprehension activities let children check their understanding by answering age-perfect questions, responding to true/false items, and drawing informative pictures.

The texts in each category increase in difficulty, giving you the flexibility to meet the needs of children at different ability levels. They are correlated with guided reading levels A–E. (See page 7 for the specific level of each story.) Each text is paired with a comprehension activity page that children complete to demonstrate their understanding of what they have read. The items include important skills, such as identifying main ideas and details, sequencing, making predictions and inferences, understanding cause and effect, and more.

You can use the texts and comprehension activities for whole-class, small group, or one-on-one comprehension instruction. The sample lesson plan (page 8) provides a framework for introducing and modeling reading in a meaningful context, as well as for after-reading discussion and completing the comprehension activities. The texts also work well as learning-center or take-home activities. Best of all, the activities support children in meeting the reading standards for Informational Text and Foundational Skills for grades K–2. (See Connecting to the Standards, page 9.)

How to Use

The texts and companion activity pages in this book are ideal for use as part of your instruction in comprehension. Research shows that comprehension instruction can help all readers including emergent and struggling readers, improve comprehension by understanding, remembering, and communicating with others about what they read. Improved comprehension also creates greater enjoyment in reading, so children will *want* to read more!

Preparing to use these texts for comprehension instruction is as easy as 1, 2, 3! Simply make copies of the selected text and comprehension activity for each child, distribute the pages, then follow the sample lesson on page 8 to guide your instruction. You'll see that the sample lesson is very similar to an interactive read-aloud in which fluent, expressive reading is modeled while teaching the reading process in a meaningful context. The steps guide you to encourage higher levels of thinking and questioning that will help children develop understanding of the text, build vocabulary and background knowledge, and make connections to prior knowledge, self, and the world.

Teaching Tips

• Prior to the lesson, preview the text to become familiar with it.

• Identify any vocabulary that might need to be introduced.

• Enlarge the text page and display it so that everyone has a clear view of the text and illustrations.

• As you ask purposeful questions, remember that "why" and "how" questions prompt deeper thinking about the meaning of the text.

• Encourage children to ask questions and share their understanding of the text.

• Invite children to retell what they just read, including facts and details.

- Work with the whole class, small groups, or individuals to complete the comprehension page. Before children begin to fill in the page, read aloud each item and have children follow along. They can then go back and work on their own.

- As needed, model how to complete the short answer and true/false section of the comprehension page.

- Allow children to dictate their responses to items on the comprehension page.

Learning Centers

Place copies of the desired text and comprehension pages in a folder. During their turn at the center, have children take a copy of each page and independently work through the text and comprehension activity. To make the activity self-checking, enlarge the answer key for the corresponding comprehension page and staple that page to the inside of the folder. When children complete the activity, they can check their responses by referring to the answer key.

Ways to Use the Texts

The texts and companion comprehension activities are ideal for the following:

- Whole-class instruction
- Small-group instruction
- One-on-one lesson
- Learning center activity
- Individual seatwork
- Take-home practice

Guided Reading Level

Correlated by a team of guided reading specialists.

Sample Lesson

Follow the steps below to provide comprehension instruction for the text of your choice.

1. Display a copy of the text page, making sure everyone can see it. Use sticky notes to cover each of the four panels on the page.

2. Point out and read the title. Ask: "What do you think this text will be about?" Encourage children to share their predictions.

3. Take a quick picture walk through the panels, but do not read the text. Reveal one panel at a time, starting with the first panel and ending with the last. This allows children to see the pictures in sequence so they can start constructing meaning.

4. Invite children to share what they know about the text topic, based on their predictions and the picture walk. This helps them relate to the text and sets the stage for making additional predictions and connections as the lesson continues. Also, introduce any unfamiliar or difficult vocabulary words from the text.

5. Read the text aloud. Use lots of expression, animation, and enthusiasm to engage children. Pause to ask purposeful questions and check children's understanding of the text and pictures, including any text features such as labels, captions, speech bubbles, and call-outs. Model a think-aloud process to encourage understanding and thinking beyond the text and to explore vocabulary. For example, "I wonder why _____"; "I think this word means _____ because _____"; and "That reminds me of _____." Invite children to share their own comments, questions, and observations during the read-aloud.

6. After reading, talk about the details and main points of the text. Encourage children to share their understanding of the text.

7. Review the comprehension page with children before having them complete it. Encourage children to write their short answer responses in complete sentences and to refer to the text to check their work. Afterward, invite them to share and discuss their responses.

First Comprehension: Nonfiction © Scholastic Inc.

Connecting to the Standards

The lessons in this book support the College and Career Readiness Anchor Standards for Reading for students in grades K–12. These broad standards, which serve as the basis of many state standards, were developed to establish rigorous educational expectations with the goal of providing students nationwide with a quality education that prepares them for college and careers. The chart below details how the lessons align with specific reading standards for literary and informational texts for students in grades K through 2.

Foundational Skills
Print Concepts

- Demonstrate understanding of the organization and basic features of print.
- Follow words from left to right, top to bottom, and page by page.
- Recognize that spoken words are represented in written language by specific sequences of letters.
- Understand that words are separated by spaces in print.
- Recognize and name all upper- and lowercase letters of the alphabet.
- Recognize the distinguishing features of a sentence (e.g., first word, capitalization, ending punctuation).

Phonics and Word Recognition

- Know and apply grade-level phonics and word analysis skills in decoding words.
- Demonstrate basic knowledge of one-to-one letter-sound correspondences.
- Associate the long and short sounds with the common spellings for the five major vowels.
- Distinguish between similarly spelled words by identifying the sounds of the letters that differ.
- Decode regularly spelled one-syllable words.
- Know final -e and common vowel team conventions for representing long vowel sounds.
- Use knowledge that every syllable must have a vowel sound to determine the number of syllables in a printed word.
- Recognize and read grade-appropriate irregularly spelled words.

Fluency

- Read emergent-reader texts with purpose and understanding.
- Read grade-level text orally with accuracy, appropriate rate, and expression on successive readings.
- Use context to confirm or self-correct word recognition and understanding, rereading as necessary.

Informational Text Skills
Key Ideas and Details

- Ask and answer questions about key details in a text.
- Identify the main topic and retell key details of a text.
- Describe the connection between two individuals, events, ideas, or pieces of information in a text.

Craft and Structure

- Ask and answer questions about unknown words in a text.
- Identify the front cover, back cover, and title page of a book.
- Name the author and illustrator of a text and define the role of each in presenting the ideas or information in a text.

Integration of Knowledge and Ideas

- Describe the relationship between illustrations and the text in which they appear (e.g., what person, place, thing, or idea in the text an illustration depicts).
- Identify the reasons an author gives to support points in a text.
- Identify basic similarities in and differences between two texts on the same topic (e.g., in illustrations, descriptions, or procedures).

Range of Reading and Level of Text Complexity

- Actively engage in group reading activities with purpose and understanding.

A Seed Grows

1

A seed needs soil to grow.

2

A seed needs water to grow.

3

A seed needs light to grow.

4

A seed needs love to grow.

Name: Fiona Meshkova

WRITE!

1. What does a seed need to grow?

Soil, water, light, love.

2. Where does a seed grow?

A seed grows in soil.

SHADE!

1. The sun makes light.

 TRUE   FALSE

2. The girl makes light.

TRUE    FALSE

DRAW!

What does a seed grow into?

Wash to Stay Healthy

1

Wash your hands
to stay healthy.

2

Wash your face
to stay healthy.

3

Wash your hair
to stay healthy.

4

Wash your body
to stay healthy.

Name: _____

WRITE!

1. What does the boy use to wash his hands?

Soap

2. Why should you wash your hands?

to stay healthy

SHADE!

1. You should use shampoo to wash your hair.

TRUE   FALSE

2. You should use shampoo to wash your face.

TRUE   (FALSE)

DRAW!

Where do you take a bath?

bath

Animal Homes

1

These are <u>birds</u>.
They <u>live</u> in a nest.

2

These are bats.
They live in a <u>cave</u>.

3

These are <u>fish</u>.
They live in a lake.

4

These are <u>people</u>.
They live in a <u>house</u>
with pets.

First Comprehension: Nonfiction © Scholastic Inc.

WRITE!

1. Which animals live in a nest?

birds

2. Which animals live in a cave?

bats

SHADE!

1. Fish live in nests.

(TRUE)   (FALSE)

2. Fish live in lakes.

(TRUE)   (FALSE)

DRAW!

Where do people and pets live?

Homs   famuli

Living Things

1

A <u>flower</u> needs food, <u>air</u>, and <u>water</u>.
It is a <u>living</u> thing.

2

A <u>butterfly</u> needs food, air, and water.
It is a living thing.

3

A kid needs food, air, and water.
It is a living thing.

4

A <u>slide</u> does NOT need food, air, and water.
It is NOT a living thing.

is NOT = (isn't) = is not

First Comprehension: Nonfiction © Scholastic Inc.

Name: _____

WRITE!

1. What do living things need?

food air water

Abutterfly ~~feet~~

2. How are a kid and a butterfly alike?

SHADE!

1. A rock is a living thing.

TRUE   FALSE

2. A flower is a living thing.

TRUE   FALSE

DRAW!

What is another living thing?

Chicken Life Cycle

1

EGG

Cluck, cluck!
A chicken lays an egg.

2

Shh, shh!
A chick grows
inside the egg.

3

Crack, crack!
A chick hatches
from the egg.

4

Peep, peep!
A chick grows up
to be a chicken!

Name: _____

WRITE!

1. What happens FIRST in the chicken life cycle?

a chicken layd an egg

2. What happens LAST in the chicken life cycle?

the chick to grows
into a chicken

SHADE!

1. A chick lays an egg.

TRUE   ~~FALSE~~

2. A chick grows inside the egg.

~~TRUE~~   FALSE

DRAW!

What hatches from an egg?

The Weather Changes

1

Some days are sunny.
The sun makes heat.
Hooray!

2

Some days are rainy.
The rain falls from clouds.
Hooray!

3

Some days are windy.
The wind blows kites.
Hooray!

4

Some days are snowy.
You can use snow
to build a snowman.
Hooray!

Name: _____

WRITE!

1. What does the wind do to kites?

maks it fli

2. What can you build with snow?

snowman

SHADE!

1. Rain falls from the sun.

(TRUE)    (FALSE)

2. Rain falls from clouds.

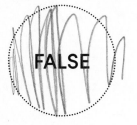 (TRUE)   (FALSE)

DRAW!

What is your favorite weather?

summr
sister
wintr
me

old
sister

Your Body Works

1

Your heart works
all the time.
It helps you stay alive.

2

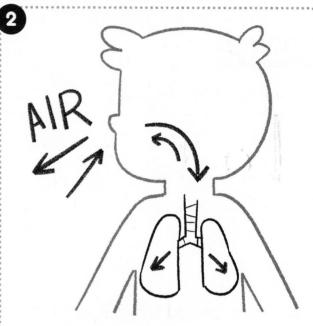

Your lungs work
all the time.
They help you breathe.

3

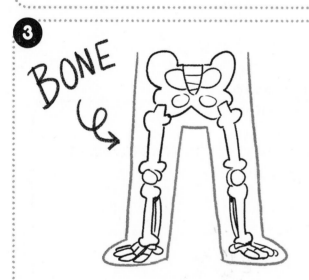

Your bones work
all the time.
They help you sit
and stand.

4

Your muscles
work all the time.
They help you run
and play!

First Comprehension: Nonfiction © Scholastic Inc.

Name: _____

WRITE!

1. Why do you need lungs?

To breath

2. Why do you need bones?

To sit and stand

SHADE!

1. You have a heart in your body.

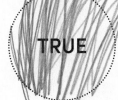 TRUE   FALSE

2. You have a star in your body.

TRUE   FALSE

DRAW!

What is something your muscles help you do?

run

Earth Goes Around

all

1

We live on a planet called Earth. Earth spins around like a top.

2

12 months = 1 year

Earth circles around the sun.

3

1 day = 24 hours

The moon circles around Earth.

4

Earth spins and circles all day and night. Around it goes!

Name: _____

WRITE!

1. What does Earth circle around?

Sun

Earth

2. What does the moon circle around?

SHADE!

1. The Earth has two moons.

(TRUE)   (FALSE)

2. The Earth has one moon.

(TRUE)   (FALSE)

DRAW!

What planet do we live on?

erth

The Water Cycle

1

Clouds fill the sky.
Rain falls from the clouds.

2

The sun comes out.
It heats the wet ground.

3

Tiny drops of water
rise up.
They are called vapor.

4

The drops grow and
form clouds.
Soon, clouds fill the sky.

Name: _Fiona Meshkova_

WRITE!

1. What forms in the sky?

Clouds forms in the sky.

2. What does the sun do in the water cycle?

The sun heats the wet ground.

SHADE!

1. Tiny drops of milk are in vapor.

TRUE   FALSE (shaded)

2. Tiny drops of water are in vapor.

TRUE (shaded)   FALSE

DRAW!

What falls from clouds?

Rain

Community Helpers

1

Doctors are helpers.

2

Police officers are helpers.

3

Firefighters are helpers.

4

Teachers are helpers. Thank you!

Name: _____

WRITE!

1. How do doctors help us?

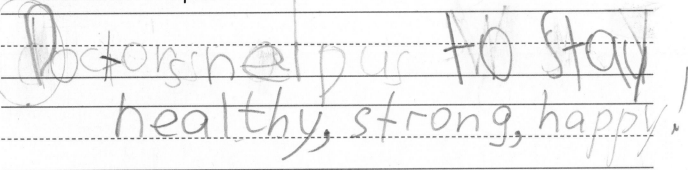

Doctors help us to stay healthy, strong, happy!

2. How do firefighters help us?

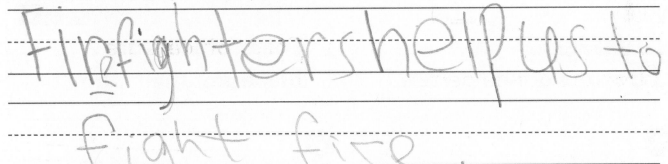

Firefighters help us to fight fire.

SHADE!

1. Police officers help us learn to read.

TRUE   ~~FALSE~~

2. Police officers help keep us safe.

~~TRUE~~   FALSE

DRAW!

Can you think of another community helper?

The First Thanksgiving

1

The pilgrims gave thanks for their homes.

2

The pilgrims gave thanks for their land.

3

The pilgrims gave thanks for their food.

4

The pilgrims gave thanks for their friends.

Name: _____

WRITE!

1. Who had the first Thanksgiving?

Pilgrims

2. Who were the Pilgrims' friends?

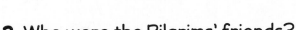

?

SHADE!

1. The Pilgrims gave thanks for their pets.

(TRUE)   (~~FALSE~~)

2. The Pilgrims gave thanks for their land.

(~~TRUE~~)   (FALSE)

DRAW!

What three foods are you thankful for?

COOKis

 PISSU

Light the Candles!

1

ADVENT WREATH

Light the candles
for Christmas.
Glow, candles, glow!

2

← SHAMASH

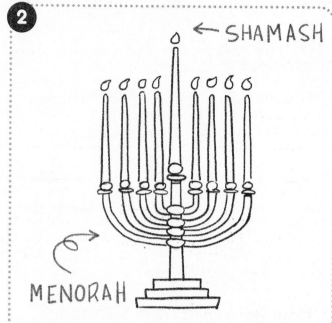

MENORAH

Light the candles
for Hanukkah.
Glow, candles, glow!

3

LUMINARIAS

Light the candles
for Las Posadas.
Glow, candles, glow!

4

KINARA

Light the candles
for Kwanzaa.
Glow, candles, glow!

WRITE!

1. How are all of these winter holidays alike?

_____

- -

_____

_____

- -

_____

2. How many candles are lit for Hanukkah?

_____

- -

_____

_____

- -

_____

SHADE!

1. Ten candles are lit for Kwanzaa.

TRUE   FALSE

2. Seven candles are lit for Kwanzaa.

TRUE   FALSE

DRAW!

How do you celebrate at holiday time?

A Loud New Year

1

We hear loud horns.
Happy New Year!

2

We hear loud drums.
Happy New Year!

3

We hear loud cheers.
Happy New Year!

4

We hear loud fireworks.
Happy New Year!

WRITE!

1. What holiday is this story about?

_____

- -

_____

- -

_____

2. What three sounds do fireworks make?

_____

- -

_____

- -

_____

SHADE!

1. The New Year is a noisy time.

TRUE   FALSE

2. The New Year is a quiet time.

TRUE   FALSE

DRAW!

What is your favorite loud thing that can be heard for the New Year?

How We Travel

1

The car goes on
the road.
Go, car, go!

2

The train goes on
the track.
Go, train, go!

3

The boat goes in
the water.
Go, boat, go!

4

The plane goes in
the sky.
Go, plane, go!

Name: _____

WRITE!

1. What goes on the road?

A car goes on the road.

2. What goes in the sky?

A plane goes in the sky.

SHADE!

1. A train travels on tracks.

(**TRUE**)   (**FALSE**)

2. A train travels on water.

(**TRUE**)   (**FALSE**)

DRAW!

What is your favorite way to travel?

Flag Day

1

Flag Day is on June 14.
Wave the flag!

2

STAR

Our flag has 50 stars.
Wave the flag!

3

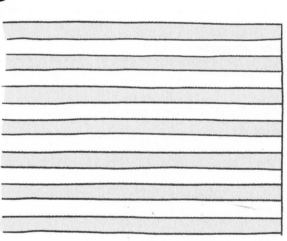

STRIPE

Our flag has 13 stripes.
Wave the flag!

4

Our flag is called the
Stars and Stripes.
Wave the flag!

First Comprehension: Nonfiction © Scholastic Inc.

Name: _____

WRITE!

1. When is Flag Day?

June 14

2. What is our flag called?

Stars and Stripes.

SHADE!

1. Our flag has 50 stars.

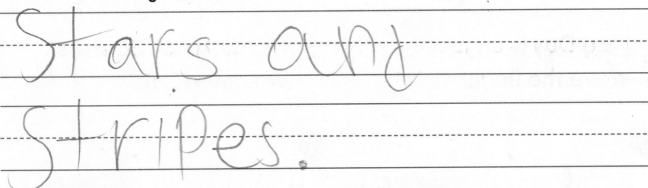

TRUE   FALSE

2. Our flag has 50 stripes.

TRUE   FALSE

DRAW!

What shapes are on our flag? Draw them.

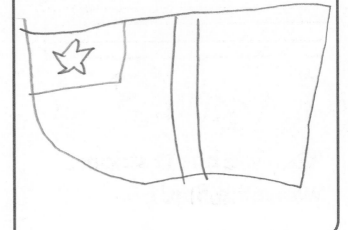

Happy Birthday, America!

1

It's July 4.
We march in parades.

2

It's July 4.
We wave flags.

3

It's July 4.
We watch fireworks.

4

It's July 4.
We celebrate America!
Happy birthday!

First Comprehension: Nonfiction © Scholastic Inc.

WRITE!

1. When is America's birthday?

_____

- - - - - - - - - - - - - - - - - - - -

_____

- - - - - - - - - - - - - - - - - - - -

2. What do we wave on July 4?

- - - - - - - - - - - - - - - - - - - -

_____

- - - - - - - - - - - - - - - - - - - -

_____

SHADE!

1. We ride in trains on July 4.

TRUE   FALSE

2. We march in parades on July 4.

TRUE   FALSE

DRAW!

What do you like to do on America's birthday?

Earth Day

1

Earth Day is a day in April.
It is a day to care for our Earth.

2

Earth Day is a day to pick up trash.
It is a day to plant trees.

3

Earth Day is a day to save water.
It is a day to recycle.

4

Earth Day is a day in April.
But we can make every day Earth Day!

Name: _____

WRITE!

1. What month is Earth Day in?

_____

_____

_____

_____

_____

2. What is one thing people do on Earth Day?

_____

_____

_____

_____

_____

SHADE!

1. We help the moon on Earth Day.

(TRUE)   (FALSE)

2. We help the Earth on Earth Day.

(TRUE)   (FALSE)

DRAW!

What is one thing you can do to care for the Earth?

Johnny Appleseed

1

Johnny Appleseed
grew apples.

2

Johnny Appleseed
picked apples.

3

Johnny Appleseed
ate apples.

4

Johnny Appleseed
shared apples.

Name: _____

WRITE!

1. What did Johnny Appleseed grow?

_____

- -

_____

_____

- -

_____

2. What did Johnny Appleseed eat?

- -

_____

_____

- -

_____

SHADE!

1. Johnny Appleseed shared his apples.

(TRUE) (FALSE)

2. Johnny Appleseed did not share his apples.

(TRUE) (FALSE)

DRAW!

What do apples grow on?

Abraham Lincoln

1

Abraham Lincoln worked at a store.

2

Abraham Lincoln worked at a post office.

3

Abraham Lincoln worked at a law office.

4

Abraham Lincoln worked at the White House.
He was our 16th president.

Name: _____

WRITE!

1. What are two places that Abraham Lincoln worked?

_____

- -

_____

_____

2. What is the most important job that Abraham Lincoln had?

_____

- -

_____

- -

SHADE!

1. Abraham Lincoln was our 1st president.

(TRUE)   (FALSE)

2. Abraham Lincoln was our 16th president.

(TRUE)   (FALSE)

DRAW!

What did Abraham Lincoln wear on his head?

Wilma Rudolph

1

Wilma loved to run.
Wilma ran in her yard.
Run, Wilma, run!

2

Wilma ran in her town.
Run, Wilma, run!

3

Wilma ran in her school.
Run, Wilma, run!

4

Wilma ran in the Olympics.
She won gold medals.
Run, Wilma, run!

WRITE!

1. What did Wilma love to do?

_____

- -

_____

_____

- -

_____

2. What are two places that Wilma ran?

_____

- -

_____

_____

- -

_____

SHADE!

1. Wilma was a fast runner.

TRUE   FALSE

2. Wilma was a slow runner.

TRUE   FALSE

DRAW!

What did Wilma win at the Olympics?

Squanto

1

Squanto helped
the Pilgrims.
He showed them
how to pick berries.

2

Squanto helped
the Pilgrims.
He showed them
how to grow corn.

3

Squanto helped
the Pilgrims.
He showed them
how to fish.

4

Squanto helped
the Pilgrims.
He showed them
how to be a good friend.

First Comprehension: Nonfiction © Scholastic Inc

WRITE!

1. Who did Squanto help?

_____

_____

_____

_____

2. How was Squanto a good friend to the Pilgrims?

_____

_____

_____

_____

SHADE!

1. Squanto showed the Pilgrims how to survive in a new land.

TRUE   FALSE

2. The Pilgrims showed Squanto how to survive in a new land.

TRUE   FALSE

DRAW!

What is something Squanto did to help the Pilgrims?

Cesar Chavez

1

Cesar Chavez was a farm worker.
He helped other farm workers.

2

This food is for you.

He helped farm workers get better food.

3

Your house will be fixed.

He helped farm workers get better homes.

4

You will make more money.

He helped farm workers get better pay.
Thank you, Cesar Chavez.

WRITE!

1. What job did Cesar Chavez have?

_____

- -

_____

_____

- -

_____

2. What are two ways Cesar Chavez helped other farm workers?

_____

- -

_____

_____

- -

SHADE!

1. This story shows a picture of Cesar Chavez picking flowers.

TRUE   FALSE

2. This story shows a picture of Cesar Chavez picking grapes.

TRUE   FALSE

DRAW!

What food grows on farms?

The Wright Brothers

1

Wilbur and Orville Wright watched birds fly.

2

The brothers wanted to fly, too.

3

The Wright Flyer in 1903

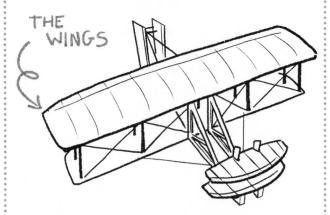

The brothers built a plane.
It had wings like a bird.

4

Airplanes Today

Their plane could fly!
Now, we can all fly.

Name: _____

WRITE!

1. What did Wilbur and Orville Wright want to do?

_____

_____

_____

_____

2. Why do you think the brothers watched birds fly?

_____

_____

_____

_____

SHADE!

1. The brothers wore wings so they could fly.

(TRUE)   (FALSE)

2. The brothers made a plane that had wings.

(TRUE)   (FALSE)

DRAW!

Besides birds, what other animals can fly?

Helen Keller

1

Helen could not hear.

Helen Keller was deaf.
She could not hear.

2

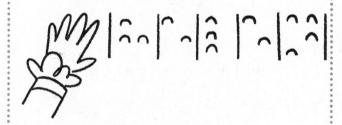

Helen Keller learned
a way to talk.
She made words with
her hands!

3

Helen could not see.

Helen Keller was blind.
She could not see.

4

Braille is a letter code made of bumpy dots

Helen Keller learned
a way to read.
She read words with
her hands!

WRITE!

1. Who is this story about?

_____

_____

_____

_____

2. Why was Helen Keller so amazing?

_____

_____

_____

_____

SHADE!

1. Blind people can learn to read braille.

TRUE   FALSE

2. Blind people can learn to read sign language.

TRUE   FALSE

DRAW!

What part of the body did Helen use to talk and read?

Martin Luther King, Jr.

1

Martin Luther King, Jr. had a dream.
He shared his dream with others.

2

Martin talked with others to share his dream.

3

Martin walked with others to share his dream.

4

Others began to share Martin's dream.
Martin received a medal for his good work!

WRITE!

1. Who had a dream for America?

_____

_____

_____

_____

2. What was Martin's dream?

_____

_____

_____

_____

SHADE!

1. Martin was a baker.

(TRUE)   (FALSE)

2. Martin was a hero.

(TRUE)   (FALSE)

DRAW!

What did Martin get for his good work?

Answer Key

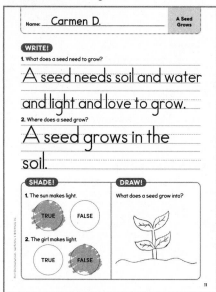

Name: **Carmen D.**   A Seed Grows

WRITE!

1. What does a seed need to grow?

A seed needs soil and water and light and love to grow.

2. Where does a seed grow?

A seed grows in the soil.

SHADE!

1. The sun makes light.   TRUE   FALSE

2. The girl makes light.   TRUE   **FALSE**

DRAW!

What does a seed grow into?

11

Name: **Carmen D.**   Wash to Stay Healthy

WRITE!

1. What does the boy use to wash his hands?

The boy uses soap to wash his hands.

2. Why should you wash your hands?

You should wash your hands to get them clean and to stay healthy.

SHADE!

1. You should use shampoo to wash your hair.   TRUE   FALSE

2. You should use shampoo to wash your face.   TRUE   **FALSE**

DRAW!

Where do you take a bath?

13

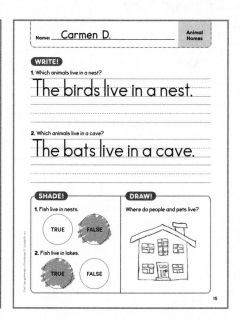

Name: **Carmen D.**   Animal Homes

WRITE!

1. Which animals live in a nest?

The birds live in a nest.

2. Which animals live in a cave?

The bats live in a cave.

SHADE!

1. Fish live in nests.   TRUE   **FALSE**

2. Fish live in lakes.   **TRUE**   FALSE

DRAW!

Where do people and pets live?

15

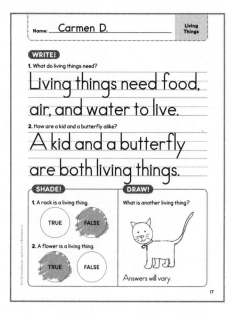

Name: **Carmen D.**   Living Things

WRITE!

1. What do living things need?

Living things need food, air, and water to live.

2. How are a kid and a butterfly alike?

A kid and a butterfly are both living things.

SHADE!

1. A rock is a living thing.   TRUE   **FALSE**

2. A flower is a living thing.   **TRUE**   FALSE

DRAW!

What is another living thing?

Answers will vary.

17

Name: **Carmen D.**   Chicken Life Cycle

WRITE!

1. What happens FIRST in the chicken life cycle?

First, a chicken lays an egg.

2. What happens LAST in the chicken life cycle?

Last, a chick grows into a chicken.

SHADE!

1. A chick lays an egg.   TRUE   **FALSE**

2. A chick grows inside the egg.   **TRUE**   FALSE

DRAW!

What hatches from an egg?

19

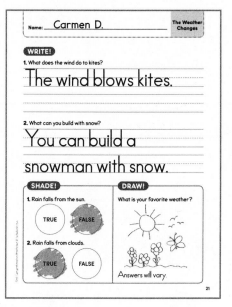

Name: **Carmen D.**   The Weather Changes

WRITE!

1. What does the wind do to kites?

The wind blows kites.

2. What can you build with snow?

You can build a snowman with snow.

SHADE!

1. Rain falls from the sun.   TRUE   **FALSE**

2. Rain falls from clouds.   **TRUE**   FALSE

DRAW!

What is your favorite weather?

Answers will vary.

21

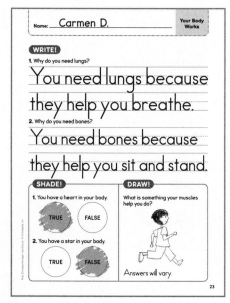

Name: **Carmen D.**   Your Body Works

WRITE!

1. Why do you need lungs?

You need lungs because they help you breathe.

2. Why do you need bones?

You need bones because they help you sit and stand.

SHADE!

1. You have a heart in your body.   **TRUE**   FALSE

2. You have a star in your body.   TRUE   **FALSE**

DRAW!

What is something your muscles help you do?

Answers will vary.

23

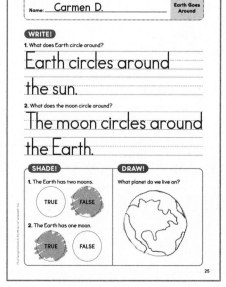

Name: **Carmen D.**   Earth Goes Around

WRITE!

1. What does Earth circle around?

Earth circles around the sun.

2. What does the moon circle around?

The moon circles around the Earth.

SHADE!

1. The Earth has two moons.   TRUE   **FALSE**

2. The Earth has one moon.   **TRUE**   FALSE

DRAW!

What planet do we live on?

25

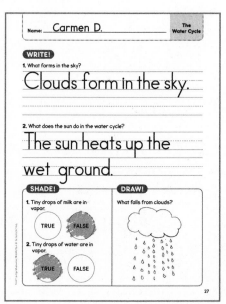

Name: **Carmen D.**   The Water Cycle

WRITE!

1. What forms in the sky?

Clouds form in the sky.

2. What does the sun do in the water cycle?

The sun heats up the wet ground.

SHADE!

1. Tiny drops of milk are in vapor.   TRUE   **FALSE**

2. Tiny drops of water are in vapor.   **TRUE**   FALSE

DRAW!

What falls from clouds?

27

Answer Key

Name: Carmen D.　　　　*Community Helpers*

WRITE!

1. How do doctors help us?

Doctors help us get better when we are sick.

2. How do firefighters help us?

Firefighters put out fires.

SHADE!

1. Police officers help us learn to read.　~~TRUE~~　**FALSE**

2. Police officers help keep us safe.　**TRUE**　FALSE

DRAW!

Can you think of another community helper?

Answers will vary.

29

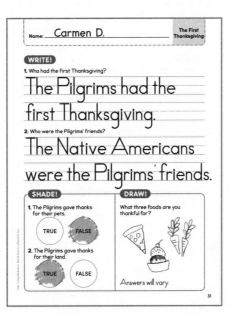

Name: Carmen D.　　　　*The First Thanksgiving*

WRITE!

1. Who had the first Thanksgiving?

The Pilgrims had the first Thanksgiving.

2. Who were the Pilgrims' friends?

The Native Americans were the Pilgrims' friends.

SHADE!

1. The Pilgrims gave thanks for their pets.　TRUE　**FALSE**

2. The Pilgrims gave thanks for their land.　**TRUE**　FALSE

DRAW!

What three foods are you thankful for?

Answers will vary.

31

Name: Carmen D.　　　　*Light the Candles!*

WRITE!

1. How are all of these winter holidays alike?

All of these winter holidays have candles.

2. How many candles are lit for Hanukkah?

Nine candles are lit for Hanukkah.

SHADE!

1. Ten candles are lit for Kwanzaa.　TRUE　**FALSE**

2. Seven candles are lit for Kwanzaa.　**TRUE**　FALSE

DRAW!

How do you celebrate at holiday time?

Answers will vary.

33

Name: Carmen D.　　　　*A Loud New Year*

WRITE!

1. What holiday is this story about?

This story is about the New Year.

2. What three sounds do fireworks make?

Fireworks make these sounds, "Bang! Boom! Pop!"

SHADE!

1. The New Year is a noisy time.　**TRUE**　FALSE

2. The New Year is a quiet time.　TRUE　**FALSE**

DRAW!

What is your favorite loud thing that can be heard for the New Year?

35

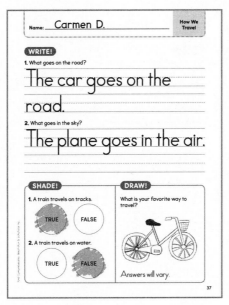

Name: Carmen D.　　　　*How We Travel*

WRITE!

1. What goes on the road?

The car goes on the road.

2. What goes in the sky?

The plane goes in the air.

SHADE!

1. A train travels on tracks.　**TRUE**　FALSE

2. A train travels on water.　TRUE　**FALSE**

DRAW!

What is your favorite way to travel?

Answers will vary.

37

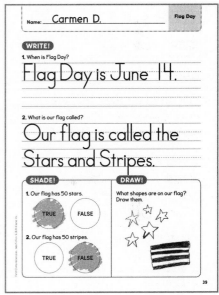

Name: Carmen D.　　　　*Flag Day*

WRITE!

1. When is Flag Day?

Flag Day is June 14.

2. What is our flag called?

Our flag is called the Stars and Stripes.

SHADE!

1. Our flag has 50 stars.　**TRUE**　FALSE

2. Our flag has 50 stripes.　TRUE　**FALSE**

DRAW!

What shapes are on our flag? Draw them.

39

Name: Carmen D.　　　　*Happy Birthday, America!*

WRITE!

1. When is America's birthday?

America's birthday is July 4th.

2. What do we wave on July 4?

We wave flags on July 4th.

SHADE!

1. We ride in trains on July 4.　TRUE　**FALSE**

2. We march in parades on July 4.　**TRUE**　FALSE

DRAW!

What do you like to do on America's birthday?

41

Name: Carmen D.　　　　*Earth Day*

WRITE!

1. What month is Earth Day in?

Earth day is in the month of April.

2. What is one thing people do on Earth Day?

People pick up trash on Earth Day.

SHADE!

1. We help the moon on Earth Day.　TRUE　**FALSE**

2. We help the Earth on Earth Day.　**TRUE**　FALSE

DRAW!

What is one thing you can do to care for the Earth?

Answers will vary.

43

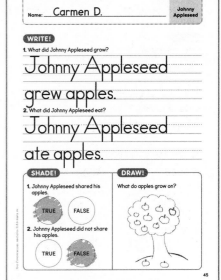

Name: Carmen D.　　　　*Johnny Appleseed*

WRITE!

1. What did Johnny Appleseed grow?

Johnny Appleseed grew apples.

2. What did Johnny Appleseed eat?

Johnny Appleseed ate apples.

SHADE!

1. Johnny Appleseed shared his apples.　**TRUE**　FALSE

2. Johnny Appleseed did not share his apples.　TRUE　**FALSE**

DRAW!

What do apples grow on?

45

Answer Key

Abraham Lincoln

Name: **Carmen D.**

WRITE!

1. What are two places that Abraham Lincoln worked?

Abraham Lincoln worked at a store and a post office.

2. What is the most important job that Abraham Lincoln had?

Abraham Lincoln was the president of the United States.

SHADE!

1. Abraham Lincoln was our 1st president.
~~TRUE~~ / FALSE

2. Abraham Lincoln was our 16th president.
TRUE / ~~FALSE~~

DRAW!

What did Abraham Lincoln wear on his head?

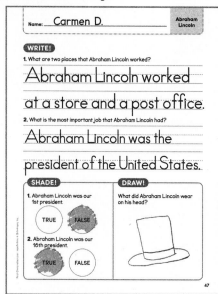

47

Wilma Rudolph

Name: **Carmen D.**

WRITE!

1. What did Wilma love to do?

Wilma loved to run!

2. What are two places that Wilma ran?

Wilma ran in her yard and in her town.

SHADE!

1. Wilma was a fast runner.
~~TRUE~~ / FALSE

2. Wilma was a slow runner.
TRUE / ~~FALSE~~

DRAW!

What did Wilma win at the Olympics?

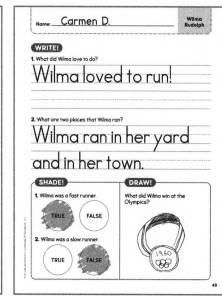

49

Squanto

Name: **Carmen D.**

WRITE!

1. Who did Squanto help?

Squanto helped the Pilgrims.

2. How was Squanto a good friend to the Pilgrims?

Squanto showed the Pilgrims how to pick berries, grow plants, and fish.

SHADE!

1. Squanto showed the Pilgrims how to survive in a new land.
~~TRUE~~ / FALSE

2. The Pilgrims showed Squanto how to survive in a new land.
TRUE / ~~FALSE~~

DRAW!

What is something Squanto did to help the Pilgrims?

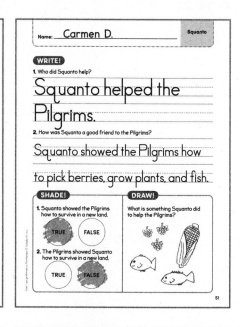

51

Cesar Chavez

Name: **Carmen D.**

WRITE!

1. What job did Cesar Chavez have?

Cesar Chavez was a farm worker.

2. What are two ways Cesar Chavez helped other farm workers?

Cesar Chavez helped other farm workers get better food and homes.

SHADE!

1. This story shows a picture of Cesar Chavez picking flowers.
TRUE / ~~FALSE~~

2. This story shows a picture of Cesar Chavez picking grapes.
~~TRUE~~ / FALSE

DRAW!

What food grows on farms?

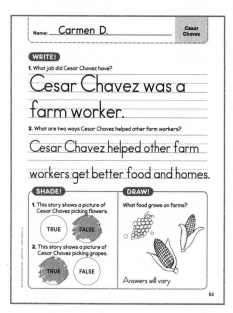

Answers will vary.

53

The Wright Brothers

Name: **Carmen D.**

WRITE!

1. What did Wilbur and Orville Wright want to do?

Wilbur and Orville Wright wanted to fly.

2. Why do you think the brothers watched birds fly?

Watching birds helped make a plane with wings that could fly.

SHADE!

1. The brothers wore wings so they could fly.
TRUE / ~~FALSE~~

2. The brothers made a plane that had wings.
~~TRUE~~ / FALSE

DRAW!

Besides birds, what other animals can fly?

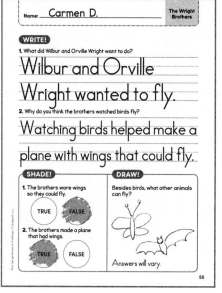

Answers will vary.

55

Helen Keller

Name: **Carmen D.**

WRITE!

1. Who is this story about?

This story is about a woman named Helen Keller.

2. Why was Helen Keller so amazing?

Helen was deaf and blind but she learned to talk and read!

SHADE!

1. Blind people can learn to read braille.
~~TRUE~~ / FALSE

2. Blind people can learn to read sign language.
TRUE / ~~FALSE~~

DRAW!

What part of the body did Helen use to talk and read?

57

Martin Luther King, Jr.

Name: **Carmen D.**

WRITE!

1. Who had a dream for America?

Martin Luther King, Jr. had a dream for America.

2. What was Martin's dream?

Martin Luther King, Jr. dreamed that all people would be treated the same.

SHADE!

1. Martin was a baker.
TRUE / ~~FALSE~~

2. Martin was a hero.
~~TRUE~~ / FALSE

DRAW!

What did Martin get for his good work?

59

Notes

Notes